Ogres and Giants

by John Hamilton

VISIT US AT

WWW.ABDOPUB.COM

Published by ABDO Publishing Company, 4940 Viking Drive, Suite 622, Edina, Minnesota 55435.

Printed in the United States.

Editor: Paul Joseph
Graphic Design: John Hamilton
Cover Design: TDI
Cover Illustration: *Idiot Fiend* ©1995 Don Maitz
Interior Photos and Illustrations: p 1 Warty Fiend ©1995 Don Maitz; p 4 *The Thief of Baghdad*, Corbis;
p 5 *Giant Wizard* ©1996 Don Maitz; p 6 *Idiot Fiend* ©1995 Don Maitz; p 7 Giant's Causeway, Corbis;
p 8 David and Goliath, Corbis; p 9 *The Colossus*, Corbis; p 11 *Titan* ©1995 Don Maitz; p 12 Thor and
Ymir, Mary Evans Picture Library; p 13 *King Kong*, Corbis; p 14 *Shrek*, courtesy Dreamworks; p 15 *Mad
Fiend* ©1995 Don Maitz; p 16 Tom Thumb and Grumbo, Mary Evans Picture Library; p 17 *Specimens
for Home* ©1977 Don Maitz; p 19 Odin riding Sleipner, Mary Evans Picutre Library; p 20 Odysseus and
Cyclops, Mary Evans Picture Library; p 21 *Cyclops* ©1995 Don Maitz; p 22 *Jack and the Giant*, Mary
Evans Picture Library; p 23 Persian giant, Corbis; p 24 Bigfoot, Corbis; p 25 Paul Bunyan, Corbis; p 27
Brave little tailor, Mary Evans Picture Library; p 28 Elephants, Corbis; p 29 *Female Titan* ©1995 Don
Maitz.

Library of Congress Cataloging-in-Publication Data

Hamilton, John, 1959–
     Ogres & giants / John Hamilton
          p. cm. — (Fantasy & folklore)
     Includes bibliographical references and index.
     ISBN 1-59197-714-2
     1. Giants. 2. Ghouls and ogres. I. Title: Ogres and giants. II. Title. III. Series: Hamilton,
John, 1959- . Fantasy & folklore.

     GR560.H35 2005
     398'.45—dc22

                                                    2004047602

CONTENTS

Fee Fi Fo Fum

iants, in one form or another, have inhabited the world's folklore and mythology since people first began telling stories. Giants are described as humanlike in appearance, but huge in stature. Sometimes they have supernatural powers. They are also stupid, savage, and cannibalistic, with a preference for human flesh and blood. They can wolf down a whole herd of cows or sheep in one sitting, or drink a river dry. They can even split a mountain in two, or chop down an entire forest with the swing of a gigantic axe.

The Welsh fairy tale *Jack and the Beanstalk* illustrates a typical giant: cruel, stupid, hostile toward humans, and a hoarder of treasures and magical objects. Heroes who conquer giants usually do so by the use of their wits, rather than brute strength.

Right: Sabu from *The Thief of Baghdad* gets caught beneath a giant's foot. *Far right:* Fantasy illustrator Don Maitz's *Giant Wizard.*

In mankind's early history, giants and other monsters, such as dragons, explained the frightening unknown. Evidence of enormous, fearful beasts could be seen in every earthquake, flood, or solar eclipse. In the days before science, it was simple to explain these natural events as the result of supernatural creatures, such as giants. Fossilized bones, which we know today are the remains of dinosaurs and other prehistoric beasts, gave further proof to early peoples that giants once roamed the earth.

To many ancient cultures, giants were beings that existed before the gods, but were eventually defeated by them. Everybody *knew* there were immense human-like creatures that once existed. Many European legends hold that people of an ancient "golden age" were gigantic of stature, but had since died out, or shrunk to today's size.

The thirteenth-century Danish author and historian Saxo Grammaticus wrote, in his famous book *The History of the Danes*, "That the Danish area was once cultivated by a civilization of giants is testified by the immense stones attached to ancient barrows and caves. If anyone is doubtful whether or not this was executed by superhuman force, let him gaze at the heights of certain mounds and then say, if he can, who carried such enormous boulders to their summits."

Above: The Giant's Causeway, in Northern Ireland, was formed millions of years ago when lava erupted from an underground fissure. Local legend says that a giant made the causeway as stepping stones to the Scottish island of Staffa.
Far left: Don Maitz's *Idiot Fiend*.

Saxo was writing about the huge stones found near some burial mounds in Denmark. Other mysterious mega-structures, including tall stone walls and gigantic earthen mounds, were said to be the work of giants from some distant, long-ago age. In reality, these rock formations, earthworks, and stone circles can be traced to Roman settlers who had occupied the region centuries earlier. To explain the ruins of these Roman construction projects, Saxo and other medieval European writers concluded that they *had* to be the result of giants. It was an obvious and simple explanation. Giants, of course, were real. Who could argue otherwise?

Giants are even mentioned in the Bible. The book of Genesis says, "There were giants in the earth in those days... ." One of the most famous stories from the Bible tells of David slaying the giant Goliath with a stone from a simple sling. Goliath was described as standing more than nine feet (2.74 m) tall, which was small for a giant, but still huge compared to a normal man.

Left: The Colossus, by Francisco Jose de Goya y Lucientes. *Far left:* David confronts the giant Goliath.

9

GIANT MYTHS

any scholars trace stories of giants to ancient Greek mythology. The term *giant* refers to Gigantes, terrible creatures with bodies of men and the legs or tails of serpents. They were the children of the goddess Gaea, who represented the earth, and Uranus, who represented the heavens. The Gigantes are often confused with the Greek Titans, but they are two different groups of creatures.

In the Greek myth *Gigantomachia*, which means "the war of the giants," the Gigantes revolted against the Olympians. The Olympians were the Greek gods who lived atop Mount Olympus. The war was desperate and bloody, but the Olympians finally defeated the Gigantes, with help from Heracles the archer. Most of the Gigantes were slain, but many were buried under mountains. According to the myth, this is why today we have earthquakes and volcanoes.

The story of the Gigantes was very popular in ancient Greek and Roman art and culture. The defeat of the giants represented the triumph of good over evil, and began the age of the Olympian gods, led by the mighty Zeus. Some of the giants, however, later emerged, including Antaeus, who built a temple out of human skulls, and Cyclops, the one-eyed giant who ate men and terrorized the land.

Far right: Don Maitz's *Titan.*

Norse mythology also has many stories of giants. Ancient Scandinavians believed that rock giants and frost giants lived in Jotunheim, a snowy land that lies on the outermost shores of the ocean. It is part of Midgard, the middle level of the Norse cosmos. One of Jutunheim's most feared inhabitants is Thrym, the dreaded frost giant whose name means "uproar." Other giants include Ymir, Utgard-Loki, Thiazi, and the giantess Menglad.

The giants of Jotunheim often battle the Norse gods. The chief enemy of the giants is Thor, the Norse god of thunder. Norse mythology says that during Ragnarok, which is the last great battle between the gods and the forces of evil, the giants will rise up and try to destroy the world.

There are many other early cultures that have myths that tell of giants. These gargantuan beings were very important in describing how the earth was first formed, sometimes by the very bodies of the giants themselves. A sampling of early giant myths includes Kua Fun and Pangu from China, Tibet's sGrolma, and Puntan of Micronesia.

Even now, during the age of science, when there seems to be a logical explanation for just about everything, stories of giants continue to fascinate people. Jonathon Swift wrote about giants in *Gulliver's Travels*. Folklore, including Germany's *Grimm's Fairy Tales,* has many stories of huge monsters. Today's modern entertainment industry has an eager audience that delights in tales of giants and ogres. From Walt Disney's *Shrek* to *King Kong*, giants seem to be everywhere.

Far left: The Norse god Thor prepares to do battle with the giant Ymir. *Below:* A publicity photo from the movie *King Kong*.

SAVAGE OGRES

Ogres are a special kind of giant from legends and fairy tales. They are fierce and cruel. They like nothing better than to feast on human flesh, especially children. Some scholars say that the word *ogre* may come from the Latin *Orcus*, who was the god of the underworld. A female ogre is called an *ogress*. Ogres are most common in the folk tales of the people of Northern Europe.

In addition to their cannibalistic nature, ogres are shy, stupid, and cowardly, much like their cousins the giants. They often have big heads, are hairy, sometimes with long beards and enormously fat bellies. Their bodies are very strong, but they have small brains. Because they have so little intelligence, ogres are easily defeated by quick-witted heroes.

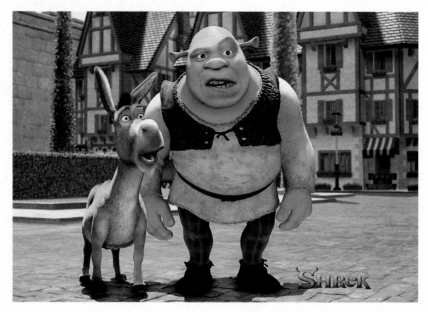

Right: Donkey and Shrek, the not-so-bloodthirsty ogre. *Far right:* Don Maitz's *Mad Fiend.*

Ogres often live in elaborate castles or palaces, usually with an abundance of riches hidden away in some secret treasure room. Sometimes an ogre's castle is built underground, or right into the side of a mountain. In Scandinavian folk tales, ogres and trolls are often interchangeable.

Children's fairy tales are full of ogres who often kidnap princesses. The seventeenth-century author Charles Perrault made the term *ogre* popular when he used these creatures in his most famous work, *Tales of Mother Goose.* Ogres have appeared in many other books, including *Tom Thumb* and *Jack and the Beanstalk.* People who study folklore say that even the witch in *Hansel and Gretel* is a kind of ogress, since she intended to devour the captive children. The Cyclops of ancient Greek mythology is also a man-eating ogre. In most of these tales, brave warriors, or even clever peasants, usually trick the dimwitted ogres, despite the monster's superior physical strength.

Left: Tom Thumb is deposited by a raven on the walls of old Grumbo the giant's castle.
Far right: Specimens for Home, by Don Maitz.

Ogre stories are usually linked to the British Isles. But one interesting explanation of the origin of the word *ogre* comes from the folklore of ancient Scandinavia. The pre-Christian Vikings believed that the world was divided into nine regions, which made up the branches, trunk, and roots of a huge "world tree" called Yggdrasil.

The Norse people believed that Odin was the ruler of the gods, who lived in the realm called Asgard. Odin's name means "All Father," but he was also the god of death. In order to gain knowledge and learn the wisdom of the dead, Odin plucked out one of his eyes and hung himself upside down from the world tree for nine days, with a spear thrust into his side. Odin died during this ordeal, and his spirit traveled the nine levels of the Norse world while riding on a magical eight-legged horse named Sleipner. During this journey he gained knowledge, plus the power of prophesy. Odin's body was later revived by three ancient, supernatural beings called the Norns.

This story helps explain why the world tree of Norse mythology is called Yggdrasil. *Yggr* means "Lord of Death." (Other sources say that Ygg stands for "the terrible one," yet another reference to Odin.) *Drasil* is a Nordic word that means both gallows (where somebody is hanged) and horse (a reference to the eight-legged Sleipner).

Up until the tenth century, the Nordic people regularly made human sacrifices to Odin, often by hanging them upside down from ash trees and thrusting spears into their sides, in the same way Odin was killed during his journey of wisdom. When Christianity finally came to Scandinavia, it swept aside the old religions. Human sacrifice was outlawed. Christian leaders compared Odin, or Yggr, with the devil.

When the old Nordic legends spread to the British Isles, the folk tales were told and retold, slowly changing over the years. Odin was transformed into a giant who lived in the clouds and ate human flesh. The Norse term for "Lord of Death," *Yggr*, eventually became *ogre,* a name for any monster that ate people.

This example of the origin of the word ogre shows just how much folk tales can change and be twisted as they are retold over generations, and pass through different cultures. In this case Odin, the wise and powerful leader of the ancient Norse gods, was transformed into a hulking, stupid, flesh-eating fiend.

Far right: Odin rides through the sky on his eight-legged horse Sleipner in this painting by Arthur Rackham.

Other Famous Giants

Cyclops

The **Cyclops** was a grotesque, man-eating giant with a single eye in the middle of his forehead. In Homer's *Odyssey*, which was written about 850 B.C., the story is told of the Greek hero Odysseus. He and his fellow warriors were captured by the Cyclops and imprisoned in a cave, where the monster began to feast on their flesh. The Cyclops became so full that he fell fast asleep. Odysseus and his men took advantage of this opportunity by stabbing the Cyclops with a sharpened spear, poking out the creature's single eye.

In agony, the blind Cyclops waited at the cave entrance to kill Odysseus and his men as they emerged. But the clever Greeks clung to the bellies of the Cyclops' sheep as they exited the cave. The Cyclops was fooled, and the Greeks narrowly escaped.

Left: Odysseus and his men make their escape from the cave of the Cyclops.
Far right: Don Maitz's *Cyclops.*

22

Left: A giant threatens three travelers from fourteenth-century Persia.
Far left: Jack and the Giant, by Richard Doyle.

Gogmagog

According to Geoffrey of Monmouth, the scholar who wrote *The History of the Kings of Britain* in 1136, **Gogmagog** was a legendary giant, 12 feet (4 m) tall, who ruled the clan of giants that inhabited the land called Albion. This was the name given to Britain before people had settled there.

Brutus, a fugitive from ancient Troy, and a band of his warriors first settled on the island and renamed it Britain. Corineus was Brutus's second in command, and one of the things he liked most was to fight giants.

When Gogmagog heard that his land had been invaded by Brutus, he rumbled across the countryside to do battle with the Trojans. As Geoffrey of Monmouth wrote in his book, "Corineus was delighted in this and threw off his armour and challenged Gogmagog to a match. The contest began. Corineus moved in and so did the giant; each caught the other by entwining his arms around the other. Gogmagog gripped Corineus with all his might and broke three ribs.

"Corineus was infuriated by what had happened and summoned all of his strength and heaved Gogmagog up on to his shoulders and, hurrying as fast as he could under his weight, ran for the nearby coast. He climbed to the top of a mighty cliff and hurled the deadly monster far out into the sea. The giant fell on the sharp rocks of the reef where he was dashed to a thousand fragments and stained the waters with his blood. The place where Corineus hurled the giant to his death is called *Gogmagog's Leap* to this day."

Paul Bunyan

Paul Bunyan is the familiar lumberjack giant of American folklore. According to legend, this gentle giant stood head and shoulders above the trees. He could chop down an entire forest with a single swing of his mighty axe. He was so big he had to use wagon wheels as buttons on his coat. When his footprints filled with water, they created Minnesota's fabled 10,000 lakes.

Many folklorists think that the tall tales of Paul Bunyan were started by lumberjacks in Minnesota, Wisconsin, and Michigan as they entertained themselves during long winter nights in the north woods. There may be a grain of truth to that. However, most experts agree that the stories we know today were actually created in 1914 by William B. Laughead. Laughead wrote stories for the Red River Lumber Company as an advertising gimmick. The stories became very popular, were expanded with outlandish characters and wild exaggerations, and soon became a part of American folklore.

Wendigo

The **Wendigo** is an ogre that inhabits the folk tales of Native American people of the United States and Canada. Wendigos were once ordinary people who became lost in the woods or trapped by winter snows. These people were forced to consume human flesh to survive. Cannibalism transformed them into giant, hideous ghouls who are forever doomed to wander the woods in search of fresh victims.

Yeti

A common form of giant in several of the world's cultures is a huge half-man, half-ape creature that wanders just outside the range of civilization. Sightings are very rare, but some evidence, such as enormous footprints, give tantalizing clues that these creatures may indeed exist. Some of these giants include the **Yeti** of Tibet, better known as the abominable snowman. There is also **Sasquatch**, or Bigfoot, of the American Pacific Northwest. **Yerin**, the Wildman of China, is another example.

Far right: An antique postcard of a man standing next to a statue of Paul Bunyan. *Below:* A photo of Bigfoot, or a man in a gorilla suit. Experts disagree.

Why Giants Can't Exist

Have you ever wondered if giants could really exist? Could the story of the Cyclops, or even King Kong, ever come true to life? Could a mad scientist, hidden away in some secret government lab, create a gigantic man or woman, perhaps by using genetic engineering? Or create a colossal bug, maybe a mosquito, by exposing it to high doses of radiation? The short answer is no.

Giants break laws. Not the kind that make it illegal to step on houses or eat children for lunch. These are laws that, once broken, threaten a creature's very existence. Giants break the laws of physics.

Specifically, giants break the dreaded *square-cube law*. This is a law that uses basic geometry. In a nutshell, the square-cube law says that objects gain mass, or weight, much faster than their surface dimensions as you scale them up.

To create a giant, you have to scale up a normal-sized person. Let's say you want a giant who is twice as tall as Michael Jordan. (Perhaps you want to create a Dream Team of supersized NBA players.) Michael Jordan stands 6-feet, 6-inches tall, and weighs 216 pounds (98 kg). Your supersized Michael Jordan would be scaled up times two, so that he stood exactly 13 feet (4 m). That's one colossal basketball player. Just think of the slam dunks!

Far right: The brave little tailor squeezes cheese, which makes the dim giant think he's squeezing water from a stone, in this painting by Arthur Rockham.

But there's a big problem: the square-cube law. Our new giant Michael Jordan stands twice as tall, but he weighs *eight times* as much, over 1,700 pounds (771 kg), almost a ton!

The square-cube law is full of advanced mathematics that you really don't have to memorize, unless you're a designer of large buildings. For fun, memorize this law of physics and repeat it to your science teacher: "While strength is proportionate to the square of the linear dimension, mass is proportionate to the cube of the linear dimension."

What this all means is that, in order for our supersized Michael Jordan to stand, he would need legs as thick and strong as an elephant's. As a matter of fact, this is exactly why elephants have such thick, strong legs, and why the giants of mythology can't exist. Giants would need bones made of titanium to even stand up. Otherwise, they would collapse under their own weight and lie there like big bags of jelly, unable to move.

Below: Elephants have thick, stocky legs in order to support their enormous weight. *Far right: Female Titan*, by Don Maitz.

Even if you could suspend the laws of physics, the laws of biology make giants an impossibility. The size and scale of internal organs, like hearts and lungs, are very dependent on the overall size of a creature. A man suddenly enlarged to the size of King Kong would quickly die, since his heart wouldn't be able to pump the massive volume of blood his organs needed, nor would his lungs be able to extract the necessary amount of oxygen from the air.

As you can see, science puts a big wet blanket on the possibility of the existence of giants. But science never stopped Hollywood from making a colossal-bug movie. Giants will always be an entertaining part of our storytelling. As long as people have a fascination with fantastic creatures, there will be stories about giants.

Glossary

ALBION

The ancient name of England, or Great Britain. Legend says that Brutus, from Troy, sailed to Albion and renamed it Britain. The name Albion is often still used in poetry.

CANNIBAL

A person who eats the flesh of other humans.

CULTURE

The behavior, arts, and beliefs of a people or group, which are passed along from generation to generation.

EXAGGERATION

To say something is bigger than it actually is, or to make something more noticeable than usual. Fishermen often exaggerate the size of the fish they catch. The tales of Paul Bunyan are filled with exaggerations, such as the claim that he was so big, he used wagon wheels for buttons.

FOLKLORE

The unwritten traditions, legends, and customs of a culture. Folklore is usually passed down by word of mouth from generation to generation.

GIMMICK

A device or idea that is used to trick or cheat people, or exaggerate the truth, such as advertising gimmicks.

LUMBERJACK

A person who cuts down trees and transports them to a lumber mill, where the wood is cut and processed. Lumberjacks are also called loggers. Paul Bunyan was a giant lumberjack.

MEDIEVAL
Something from the Middle Ages.

MIDDLE AGES
In European history, a period defined by historians as between 476 A.D. and 1450 A.D.

MYTHOLOGY
The study or collection of myths. Myths are traditional stories collected by a culture. Their authors are almost always unknown. Myths explain the origin of mankind, or of civilizations. They also explain the customs or religions of a people. Myths are often stories that include the deeds of gods and great heroes.

OLYMPIANS
In ancient Greek mythology, the Olympians were the greater gods and goddesses who lived high atop Mount Olympus. Some of the Greek gods included Ares, Apollo, Athena and Poseidon. The supreme ruler of the gods was Zeus.

PHYSICS
The science that explores the properties and changes of matter and energy. The study of electricity, optics, mechanics, and atomic energy deal with physics.

PROPHECY
A prediction of the future. Prophecies are often declared by somebody who claims to have direct guidance from a god or spirit.

STATURE
Stature is the height of a person in their natural standing position. High stature can also mean that someone is held in high regard, or well respected, by other people.

TITANS
The Titans were an ancient race of giant gods who were overthrown by the Greek gods of Olympus.

INDEX